Ten Poems
about Hats

Candlestick Press

Published by:
Candlestick Press,
Diversity House, 72 Nottingham Road, Arnold, Nottingham NG5 6LF
www.candlestickpress.co.uk

Design and typesetting by Craig Twigg

Printed by Bayliss Printing Company Ltd of Worksop, UK

Selection and Introduction © Katharine Towers, 2024

Cover illustration © Jane Burn, 2024
https://janeburnpoet.wordpress.com/

Candlestick Press monogram © Barbara Shaw, 2008

© Candlestick Press, 2024

ISBN 978 1 913627 33 1

Acknowledgements

The poems in this pamphlet are reprinted from the following books, all by permission of the publishers listed unless stated otherwise. Every effort has been made to trace the copyright holders of the poems published in this book. The editor and publisher apologise if any material has been included without permission, or without the appropriate acknowledgement, and would be glad to be told of anyone who has not been consulted.

Thanks are due to all the copyright holders cited below for their kind permission.

Rita Dove, *Collected Poems: 1974-2004* (WW Norton, 1986) Copyright © 1986 by Rita Dove. Used by permission of WW Norton & Company, Inc. John Foggin, *Pressed for Time* (Calder Valley Poetry, 2022) by kind permission of the author and publisher. John Freeman, *What Possessed Me* (Worple Press, 2016). Clarinda Harriss, *Innumerable Moons* (Beignet Press, 2019). Robert Hedin, *At the Great Door of Morning: Selected Poems and Translations* (Copper Canyon Press, 2017). Copyright 2017 by Robert Hedin. Reprinted by permission of the author. Linda Pastan, *Heroes in Disguise* (WW Norton, 1991) Copyright © 1991 by Linda Pastan. Used by permission of WW Norton & Company, Inc. and the Estate of Linda Pastan in care of the Jean V. Naggar Literary Agency, Inc. (permissions@jvnla.com). Carole Satyamurti, *The Hopeful Hat* (Bloodaxe Books, 2023) www.bloodaxebooks.com. James Tate, *Reckoner* (Wesleyan University Press, 1986). Copyright © 1986 by James Tate. Reprinted with permission. Andrew Taylor, *Collected Poems* (Salt, 2004). ASJ Tessimond, *Collected Poems* (Bloodaxe Books, 2010) www.bloodaxebooks.com.

All permissions cleared courtesy of Dr Suzanne Fairless-Aitken
c/o Swift Permissions swiftpermissions@gmail.com

Where poets are no longer living, their dates are given.

Contents

Introduction

There's something rather nostalgic about a hat – unless it happens to be a beanie or a baseball cap. *Bowler, fedora, panama, boater...* the names are a lovely litany in themselves.

In these ten poems, you'll find all sorts of head-wear – ranging from a grandfather's beloved trilby which creates a wonderful sense of occasion to a commuter's bowler which stands for "the unnoticed, the unnoticeable man" on the same train every morning.

The selection opens with John Foggin's atmospheric celebration of a milliner's shop – surely a place that deserves to be captured in a poem before there are no more left. The poem delights in details of haberdashery and in the bits and bobs a milliner uses to shape and pin and snip. The poem is a tender miniature but it evokes a whole world.

At the heart of the selection is Carole Satyamurti's eloquent 'The Hopeful Hat' about a hat waiting for coins on a city street. The encounter sparks a wry meditation on Englishness and embarrassment and regret. Elsewhere, the mood takes a surreal turn in a prose poem which imagines Napoleon's bathing cap. There's also a child's-eye view of the love between parents, encapsulated in a father's delight as a mother puts on a hat for a special occasion.

The poems range widely in mood and theme – showing that there's far more to a hat than merely something you put on your head. In some ways, we are defined by the hats that we wear. In others, a hat can be an opportunity to imagine an alternative life for ourselves – even a life in a different gender. We hope you enjoy the quirky, tender and moving poems in this little hat box.

Katharine Towers

Cloche

I think I would have liked, just once, a fitting at a milliner's,
a jumbled space, a comfortably fussy woman
with small scissors, pins between pursed lips, and wisps
of hair escaping, wayward, from a bun.
I think she's wearing black,
a cameo brooch and a touch of rouge.
I think she smells of Parma Violets, Cussons talcum powder.
There are multi-coloured reels, ends of rickrack, bias bindings,
tiny satin flowers, and hats with floppy brims
on blank-faced, long-necked Nefertiti heads,
and lots of little drawers, gilt mirrors, and a hush,
and I want a cloche in soft velour, dove-grey or dusty-pink,
and a deep, deep violet band, and one white linen rose.

I think I would have relished that.

John Foggin (1943 – 2023)

The Hat Lady

In a childhood of hats –
my uncles in homburgs and derbies,
Fred Astaire in high black silk,
the yarmulke my grandfather wore
like the palm of a hand
cradling the back of his head –
only my father went hatless,
even in winter.

And in the spring,
when a turban of leaves appeared
on every tree, the Hat Lady came
with a fan of pins in her mouth
and pins in her sleeves,
the Hat Lady came –
that Saint Sebastian of pins,
to measure my mother's head.

I remember a hat of dove-grey felt
that settled like a bird
on the nest of my mother's hair.
I remember a pillbox that tilted
over one eye – pure Myrna Loy,
and a navy straw with cherries caught
at the brim that seemed real enough
for a child to want to pick.

Last year when the chemicals
took my mother's hair, she wrapped
a towel around her head. And the Hat Lady came,
a bracelet of needles on each arm,
and led her to a place
where my father and grandfather waited,
head to bare head, and Death
winked at her and tipped his cap.

Linda Pastan (1932 – 2023)

My Grandfather's Hat

Most of the time I saw Granddad indoors,
first in his dark room with blue gas mantles
and a kitchen range and one tall window
in Poplar, then in the overheated lounge
of Aunt Nell and Uncle George's new flat
in Morden when he was in his nineties.
But he came to stay in our house sometimes,
and it must have been when he was leaving
that I saw him wearing his trilby hat.
It was grey and sleek like a new plush toy.
No one had ever made our two front steps
more like a staircase in a stately home,
not even Mum with her polio feet.
Crowning himself slowly, his own archbishop,
holding on to a handrail like a sceptre,
he turned with no more haste than one of the ships
he had sailed in round Cape Horn as a boy
in another century, approached each step
like a descent to be addressed with ropes.
Grandly he lowered one foot, then the other,
while we watched him, silently exclaiming
vivat, and the black and white chess-board
of the path to the front gate stretched out,
like a long drive lined with waving flags.

John Freeman

The man in the bowler hat

I am the unnoticed, the unnoticeable man:
The man who sat on your right in the morning train:
The man you looked through like a windowpane:
The man who was the colour of the carriage, the colour of the mounting
Morning pipe smoke.

I am the man too busy with a living to live,
Too hurried and worried to see and smell and touch:
The man who is patient too long and obeys too much
And wishes too softly and seldom.

I am the man they call the nation's backbone,
Who am boneless – playable catgut, pliable clay:
The Man they label Little lest one day
I dare to grow.

I am the rails on which the moment passes,
The megaphone for many words and voices:
I am graph, diagram,
Composite face.

I am the led, the easily-fed,
The tool, the not-quite-fool,
The would-be-safe-and-sound,
The uncomplaining bound,
The dust fine-ground,
Stone-for-a-statue waveworn pebble-round.

ASJ Tessimond (1902 – 1962)

Straw Hat

In the city, under the saw-toothed leaves of an oak
overlooking the tracks, he sits out
the last minutes before dawn, lucky
to sleep third shift. Years before
he was anything, he lay on
so many kinds of grass, under stars,
the moon's bald eye opposing.

He used to sleep like a glass of water
held up in the hand of a very young girl.
Then he learned he wasn't perfect, that
no one was perfect. So he made his way
North under the bland roof of a tent
too small for even his lean body.

The mattress ticking he shares in the work barracks
is brown and smells
from the sweat of two other men.
One of them chews snuff:
he's never met either.
To him, work is a narrow grief
and the music afterwards
is like a woman
reaching into his chest
to spread it around. When he sings

he closes his eyes.
He never knows when she'll be coming
but when she leaves, he always
tips his hat.

Rita Dove

The Hopeful Hat

At the bus stop, a dishevelled woman
in drab clothing much too big for her,
is blowing a bright pink descant recorder.
Beside her, on the ground, a hopeful hat.

Staring straight ahead, she blows 'toot toot',
child-like, flat, a mournful open note
over and over, the sound short as her breath.
I pass her several times across the morning.

The smug Victorian clock tower marks the quarters.
Still she blows 'toot toot', the dreary, stubborn
single note, dying as her breath fails.
The hat holds few coins. I think to speak to her,

ask how it has come to this, standing here
beside her hopeful hat; and could she not
manage at least one tune, like the gypsy
near Tesco – even if the rhythm's wrong?

I don't of course, restrained by that endemic
English malady, embarrassment.
Her one hopeless note follows me home,
and here I write my shabby conscience out.

Carole Satyamurti (1939 – 2019)

The List of Famous Hats

Napoleon's hat is an obvious choice I guess to list as a famous hat, but that's not the hat I have in mind. That was his hat for show. I am thinking of his private bathing cap, which in all honesty wasn't much different than the one any jerk might buy at a corner drugstore now, except for two minor eccentricities. The first one isn't even funny: Simply it was a white rubber bathing cap, but too small. Napoleon led such a hectic life ever since his childhood, even farther back than that, that he never had a chance to buy a new bathing cap and still as a grown-up – well, he didn't really grow that much, but his head did: He was a pin-head at birth, and he used, until his death really, the same little tiny bathing cap that he was born in, and this meant that later it was very painful to him and gave him many headaches, as if he needed more. So, he had to vaseline his skull like crazy to even get the thing on. The second eccentricity was that it was a *tricorn* bathing cap. Scholars like to make a lot out of this, and it would be easy to do. My theory is simple-minded to be sure: that beneath his public head there was another head and it was a pyramid or something.

James Tate (1943 – 2015)

Hat

This little roof
this portable indoors

this humidicrib of sweat
this verandah of flies

this extension of horse racing
this antique doffer to ladies

has melted down the neck
of the baseball cap generation

Andrew Taylor

The Tragedy of Hats

is that you can never see the one you're wearing,
that no one believes the lies they tell,
that they grow to be more famous than you,
that you could die in one but you won't be buried in it.

That we use them to create dogs
in our own image. That the dogs
in their mortarboards and baseball caps and veils
crush our hubris with their unconcern.

That Norma Desmond's flirty cocktail hat flung aside
left a cowlick that doomed her. That two old ladies
catfighting in Hutzler's Better Dresses both wore flowered
straw. Of my grandmother the amateur hatmaker,

this legend: that the holdup man at the Mercantile
turned to say Madam I love your hat before
he shot the teller dead who'd giggled at her
homemade velvet roses. O happy tragedy of hats!

That they make us mimic classic gestures,
inspiring pleasure first, then pity and then fear.
See how we tip them, hold them prettily against the wind
or pull them off and mop our sweaty brows

like our beloved foolish dead in photographs.
Like farmers plowing under the ancient sun.

Clarinda Harriss

My Mother's Hats

She kept them high on the top shelf,
In boxes big as drums –

Bright, crescent-shaped boats
With little fishnets dangling down –

And wore them with her best dress
To teas, coffee parties, department stores.

What a lovely catch, my father used to say,
Watching her sail off into the afternoon waters.

Robert Hedin